No graphic, visual, electronic, film, microfilm, tape recording, or any other means may be
used to reproduce in any form, without prior written permission of the author, except in the
case of brief passages embodied in critical reviews and articles.

ISBN 978-1-943521-37-1

Boyack, Connor, author.
Stanfield, Elijah, illustrator.
The Tuttle Twins and the Education Vacation / Connor Boyack.

Cover design by Elijah Stanfield
Edited and typeset by Connor Boyack

Printed in the United States

To John Taylor Gatto

For a lifetime
of learning.

"Why does this have a grade on it?" Ethan asked, pointing to the chicken in their shopping cart.

"Hey, the eggs are also graded," Emily chimed in, reading the "Grade A" label on the carton.

"Grading is common for meat, milk, and eggs," Mrs. Tuttle replied. "The grade indicates the quality."

"I wonder if the animals had to do homework like us to get good grades..." Ethan sarcastically said.

"Don't remind me about having to do homework," Emily responded, letting out a slow sigh.

Summer was flying by—and that meant they would be going back to school soon.

The twins had been having an incredible summer. At camp, Chief Ron had taught them the importance of the Golden Rule.

Then they had an awesome time at the circus that passed through town, learning to be clowns.

And best of all, they had started up a new family business, turning Nana's old dance studio into a new community theater.

As Mrs. Tuttle began unloading items from the cart onto the conveyor belt, Ethan and Emily couldn't help but feel that the hours sitting at a desk, the textbooks, and the homework that soon awaited them wouldn't be nearly as interesting or enjoyable.

"We're home!" Mrs. Tuttle announced as she and the twins walked in carrying the groceries.

"Oops! Sorry, honey," she quickly whispered. Mr. Tuttle was on a phone call and his conversation seemed important.

"I think it would be a great experience for us," Mr. Tuttle said. "I'll talk it over with them and we will

see you soon." He ended the call and came over to help with the groceries.

"What was that about, Dad?" Emily asked, grunting as she heaved a bag onto the counter.

Mr. Tuttle hummed to himself, enjoying the suspense. He walked to his office and the others followed, impatiently waiting for him to spill the beans.

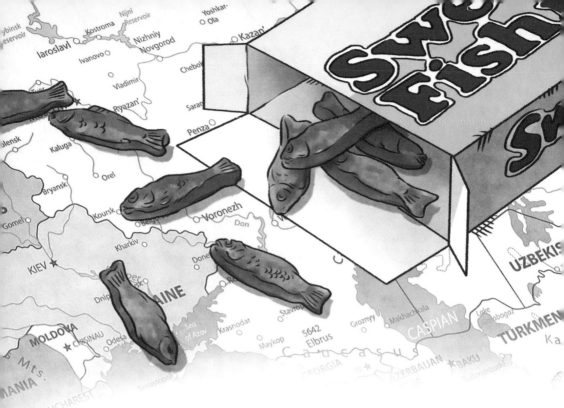

"This morning, I was invited to speak at a conference in Sweden in September," he revealed. "And I think you should all come with me! We could take a few weeks and tour some of Europe together."

"What?!" the rest of the family shouted at once, trying to take in what he had just said.

Mr. Tuttle unfolded a large map and opened a box of Swedish Fishies for them to snack on while he marked spots where he wanted to take the family.

"So, what do you think?" he asked.

"But what about school? Won't we fall behind and get bad grades?" Emily wondered. "I don't want to do catch-up homework—I get enough as it is!"

"A few weeks is a lot to miss out on," Ethan agreed, sounding anxious. "If I don't do well in school, I might not get into the college I want, or get a good job when I'm older... I've got a future to think about!"

"Honey, I don't think the school will let them take that much time off," Mrs. Tuttle said. "There are laws about that. You and I could even get in trouble."

"I understand your concerns," Mr. Tuttle reassured them. "That's why I called Mrs. Miner just now."

"Oh?" Mrs. Tuttle replied. "What did she say?"

"She invited us to see a friend of hers speak at the college campus," he said. "Apparently he has written books about better ways to help children learn. She thinks it will help resolve any worries about the twins missing that much school."

A few days later, the Tuttle family picked up Mrs. Miner on their way to the event.

"I think you're all really going to like my friend," she said. "His name is John, and for most of his life he was a teacher, like me."

"He even got an award for being the 'Best Teacher' in the whole state of New York," she added, pulling a document from her bag.

"What's interesting is that the same year he got that award, he wrote this article for a national newspaper where he announced he was quitting."

"Why did he quit if he was such a good teacher?" Ethan asked.

"That's what he's going to talk about," Mrs. Miner replied. "In the article he explained that because of the way schools are set up, children can sometimes be hurt instead of helped."

"But you haven't hurt us!" Emily exclaimed.

"Other than that one low grade I got last year..." Ethan added, laughing to himself.

"You're a great teacher!" Emily said, ignoring him.

"That's very kind of you," Mrs. Miner replied, her cheeks turning red. "But I'll be honest—it's hard. Schools add so many restrictions on what teachers can do... The system doesn't really allow me to help each of you kids pursue your unique passions and interests. We're told to teach the same thing to everybody in the same way. And sometimes, a good teacher like John just quits, because it's frustrating to understand what's best for each child but not be able to do it."

The auditorium parking lot was packed with cars. "It appears your friend is popular," Mr. Tuttle remarked.

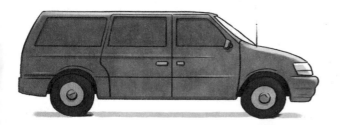

"What does that sign mean?" Emily asked as they walked toward the main building.

"*Compulsory education* is when the government forces children to go to school, or forces their parents to teach them certain things in a certain way," Mrs. Tuttle answered. "Until just a few decades ago it was even illegal to homeschool in some states... and in some countries, it still is."

"Parents get in trouble if their kids aren't taught the way the government wants?" Ethan asked.

"Yes, the government might take the children from their home or the parents might be put in jail," Mr. Tuttle said. "Crazy, right?"

"I love learning but it seems really weird to force people to do it a certain way," Emily said. "It's like the government thinks all the kids belong to them and not to their parents."

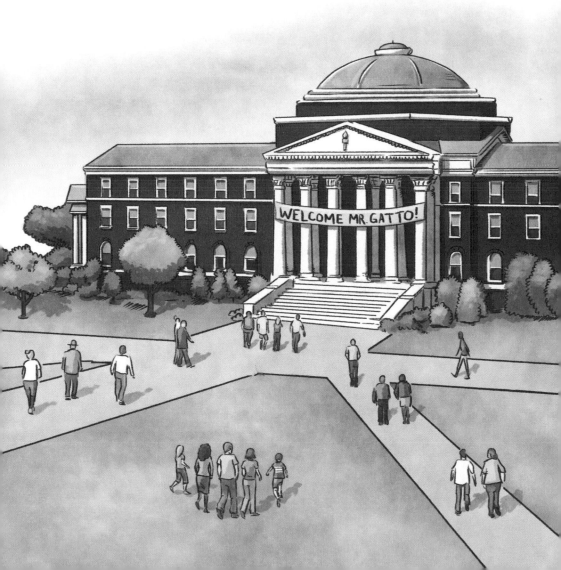

The room was packed, but Mrs. Miner had seats reserved for them on the front row. Soon after they sat down, an older man with a jolly smile and white hair was introduced at the podium.

"We all want children to succeed," Mr. Gatto said, beginning his remarks. "The question is whether compulsory education adequately does the job."

"I once thought that we could improve the education system by paying teachers more," he continued, "or by changing our *curriculum*—the

lessons and activities taught in class. By doing these things, I thought, surely my students would learn better—and not just learn, but really remember and value what I taught them."

"But I was wrong," he added slowly, emphasizing his words. "Tonight I will explain why I believe that compulsory education can harm children—and why it cannot be fixed."

"First, I need a couple of volunteers..." Mr. Gatto said, surveying the crowd.

The Tuttle twins shot their hands up eagerly, catching his attention. "Okay, how about these two up front?"

Ethan and Emily jumped onto the stage. Mr. Gatto invited them to share all the ways they were different—their favorite foods, hobbies, and interests. It was a long list!

"Now, Ethan," Mr. Gatto then asked, "if you had the freedom to control your own education, what would you want to learn and become an expert in?"

"I like making comic books, and would love to learn from a professional illustrator," he replied after some thought. "Oh, and I'm good at math and want to learn how to crack codes, but I don't think they teach how to do that in school."

"And you, Emily?" Mr. Gatto asked.

"I would spend way more time learning about science and the human body," she replied. "The health class at school is really basic, so if I was in charge, I would learn much more advanced stuff."

"My young friends here are clearly very different individuals. Wouldn't you all agree?" Mr. Gatto asked the audience.

"After many years teaching, I realized how strange it was to treat unique children like a product on a factory *conveyor belt*," he said. "Instead of helping them reach their own potential, we have instead created an elaborate education system that treats them all the same."

"They are all taught the same information, and are expected to learn in the same way. After a few minutes of learning one thing, a bell rings—then they have to move on to the next subject together, even if they wanted to keep learning more or were struggling to understand."

"This system is not natural," he added, "and it extinguishes a child's natural desire to learn. It's no wonder so many children dread school work."

"Not only are children produced to be the same, they are also inspected, graded, and sorted like we do with meat and eggs," he said, placing funny hats onto the twins' heads to illustrate what he was saying. "While rating our food makes sense, it *doesn't* make sense to grade children!"

Mrs. Tuttle leaned over to Mrs. Miner. "I remember not liking writing assignments because I always got poor grades," she said. "But after I graduated, I loved writing about things I was interested in and have even been published in a few magazines."

"Perhaps you didn't like writing *because* of the bad grades," she replied. "For some children, a bad grade makes them feel like they're not smart—like they're a bad egg that can't be used."

"Grading a child's learning is truly a strange practice," Mr. Gatto continued. "If the goal is for a child to fully understand a subject, a lower grade only shows they have not mastered it yet. Why move them on to the next chapter? Why even grade them at all? Let them learn until they understand, without discouragement."

The twins returned to their seats, and while Mr. Gatto continued speaking, Emily was lost in thought. "What's on your mind?" Mrs. Tuttle whispered to her.

Emily held out the notepad, pointing with her pencil to what she had just written.

I don't want to learn just to get good grades. I want to learn because the world is interesting. I want to understand it and help make it better.

Mrs. Tuttle reached her arm around Emily, giving her a quick squeeze. "I love that," she told her quietly. "And I agree!"

A big THUD reverberated in the room as Mr. Gatto dropped a block of something on the podium.

"It's clay!" Emily whispered. She loved doing arts and crafts and her fingers itched to start molding it. Mr. Gatto quickly began shaping the clay.

"Listen to the words of John Dewey, one of the creators of today's school system," he continued.

"Teachers are engaged, not simply in training individuals," he read. "They are social servants set apart for the maintenance of proper social order."

"I hope this alarms you," Mr. Gatto said, revealing a clay child he had formed. "People like Dewey want *conformity*—your unique children becoming the same. And they created a system to mold children, like clay, into their idea of the proper social order."

"I don't like the sound of that," Mr. Tuttle whispered toward Mrs. Tuttle. "We send our kids to school to gain knowledge, not to be taught a 'proper social order.' That's our job as their parents."

"At school, these little minds are filled with ideas," Mr. Gatto said, "but whose ideas are they? And what are the motives of those in charge?"

Ethan didn't like the idea that he was being shaped into what somebody else wanted. "I want to become my own person and learn what I want," he wrote in his notepad. "I am nobody's clay."

"Dewey modeled our modern schools after the system used in old Prussia—a militaristic nation that is now Germany," Mr. Gatto explained. "The purpose wasn't to help young people be independent thinkers, but to make them into submissive workers, soldiers, and citizens—to be more easily controlled."

"This method was so effective it was soon adopted by most governments," he added, lifting up a stack of books to the podium.

"I collect textbooks from around the world. And you know what I've found? These governments leave out important history they don't want their young people learning about."

Chatter broke out in the audience as they saw the examples Mr. Gatto was displaying. "Well, that's not sneaky..." Emily whispered sarcastically.

"It's not a good education," Ethan replied. "If we only hear the twisted version of history, we can't learn from what really happened."

"There's a name for that," Mr. Tuttle whispered. "That's not education at all—it's *propaganda*."

"It's more than that," Mrs. Tuttle added. "It seems more like *social engineering*—molding people's children to change society the way they want. I guess that's what that Dewey fellow was after."

"So you see, compulsory education hasn't really failed," Mr. Gatto concluded. "It has actually succeeded in undermining the individuality and free will of children—just as it was designed to do."

"Parents: you can do something about it, but it requires a shift in thinking," he said, holding up a tiny object. "Look closely at this seed, because it contains the lesson you should not forget."

"Education is an organic process," Mr. Gatto continued. "We can't predict how people learn best, or even what they might want to learn—just as you

don't know what this seed will become." He then pushed the seed into a small pot of soil.

"But just like any gardener knows, if we focus on creating the right conditions, a healthy plant—or child—can flourish all on its own and reveal to the world what it was destined to become."

Applause erupted as Mr. Gatto took a humble bow, giving a quick wink at the twins. Mrs. Miner smiled as she saw the reaction on the faces of Mr. and Mrs. Tuttle—it was like a light bulb had gone off inside their heads.

After the event, Mrs. Miner introduced the Tuttle family to Mr. Gatto. "I feel like I'm the one who needs to do homework now," Mrs. Tuttle said, holding one of the books she had purchased.

"Just remember this," Mr. Gatto said, handing Emily the pot he had used in his presentation. "The key to true learning is *free will*—the ability to choose your own path and learn what matters to you. When education is compulsory, there is no choice."

"Mr. Gatto, now I get why you quit," Ethan said. "It must be hard to be a school teacher—trying to help each kid in a different way, but having to grade them as if they're all supposed to be the same."

"It is very difficult," Mrs. Miner agreed. "But I feel called to stay, and do the best I can to encourage each student to follow their own interests, and get them out to explore and understand the world."

"So that's why you take us on so many field trips," Emily said, giving her a high five. "Thank you!"

COMPULSION

FREE WILL

On a rainy morning a few weeks later, the twins peered out the window as their friends lined up for the school bus on the first day of class.

"I'm excited to go on this trip," Ethan said, "but I sort of I feel like I'm missing out by not going with them."

"I know what you mean," Emily replied, nodding slowly. "The best part about school is hanging out with my friends."

"But that's not why we send you there, silly," Mrs. Tuttle commented.

Suitcases were stacked in the family room, ready to follow the Tuttle family to Europe that evening. Mrs. Tuttle nervously went over her checklist three times to be certain everything was packed, and made sure to leave instructions for their neighbor Fred who would be taking care of the house and watering the plants, including Mr. Gatto's mysterious plant that had just begun to blossom.

Mr. and Mrs. Tuttle had decided to give Mr. Gatto's ideas a try and use the vacation as an opportunity to start a new education adventure.

"Are you ready for this?" Mr. Tuttle whispered as the plane's low rumble quickly put the twins to sleep. "It's a pretty big decision."

"That's why I love the example of the plant," she replied. "It's not our job to teach everything. We just have to provide them with the right environment

and resources to learn and develop on their own—
in a way that makes the most sense to them."

"And I'm realizing something," she added. "Our
children learn the same way we do."

"You and I don't sit and wait for someone else
to decide what we should know. We explore our
curiosity. That's what I want for our kids!"

"Me, too," Mr. Tuttle replied, smiling in satisfaction.

London was a beautiful city that Ethan and Emily absolutely loved though it took a while getting used to driving on the other side of the road.

In the Natural History Museum, the twins spent hours exploring different exhibits. Emily especially loved learning about all the animals. Ethan was focused on the dinosaurs and really old rocks.

The family next visited Parliament and learned about their government. They were able to watch the House of Lords debate whether they should restrict people's ability to buy knives because some people had used them to hurt others.

The following morning, they visited Westminster Abbey, an old religious building that contains over a thousand years of history with paintings, stained glass, books, and more to see.

"I feel like I could spend a month in here and still not see everything!" Emily remarked.

Ethan nodded in agreement. "I had no idea any of this even existed," he added.

Paris was an adventure all on its own. The family was excited to spend some time in the Louvre, a famous museum with 35,000 pieces of art. Emily walked from one display to the next, using an audio guide to learn about the different pieces.

"Look, it's the real Mona Lisa!" Ethan called out. "Did you know that Leonardo da Vinci used over 30 layers of paint?"

"He was a gifted artist, for sure," Mrs. Tuttle said. "He was also an inventor—a real Renaissance man. We'll visit his birthplace in Italy in a few days."

Ethan was captivated by the painting, wondering how long da Vinci practiced to become so talented.

The rest of their time in Paris was spent visiting the Eiffel Tower and the Arc de Triomphe, which Napoleon had built to celebrate his military might and France's power.

"My feet are sore!" Ethan said, rubbing them as the family sat down at a Parisian café. "But it feels like my mind is even more sore—there's so many amazing things to learn about."

"There are also amazing things to eat," Emily said, breathing in the sweet aroma of her colorful macarons. "And they smell a lot better than your stinky feet!"

The Colosseum in Rome was much bigger than any of the Tuttles had anticipated. They imagined what it must have looked like filled with people watching the gladiators in battle.

"Dad, listen!" Ethan said. "This sign says that over half a million people lost their lives fighting animals and other people in the arena."

"And it was built by thousands of Jewish slaves," Mr. Tuttle added. "That shows how a lot of history is ugly, but we learn about it to try and be better."

"Too bad they don't give away free food anymore," Emily said as she and Mrs. Tuttle returned from a tour. "Our tour guide said that the Roman audience was fed during events to keep everybody happy and distracted so they wouldn't pay attention to the bad things their government was doing."

"Now there's a lesson we can certainly learn from," Mr. Tuttle replied.

"How could anyone think something so horrible was fun to watch?" Ethan asked, shaking his head.

"We're finally here!" Ethan shouted as they later approached the museum in Tuscany that featured the work of Leonardo da Vinci.

Hours passed quickly as the twins found themselves immersed in all sorts of gadgets and ideas that one man had created.

Ethan loved seeing the notes and sketches of the countless inventions that he thought up—including many that couldn't be made in the early 1500s since the technology to build them didn't yet exist.

"These drawings of the human anatomy are so amazing!" Emily said, admiring his drawings. "He must have spent ages studying bodies."

"The Renaissance was a period in history where there was an explosion of creativity and learning," Mrs. Tuttle explained. "Many great people, like da Vinci, changed the course of history in positive ways with their new ideas and inventions."

"That's exactly what I'm going to do!" Emily said. "It's time for a re-Renaissance!"

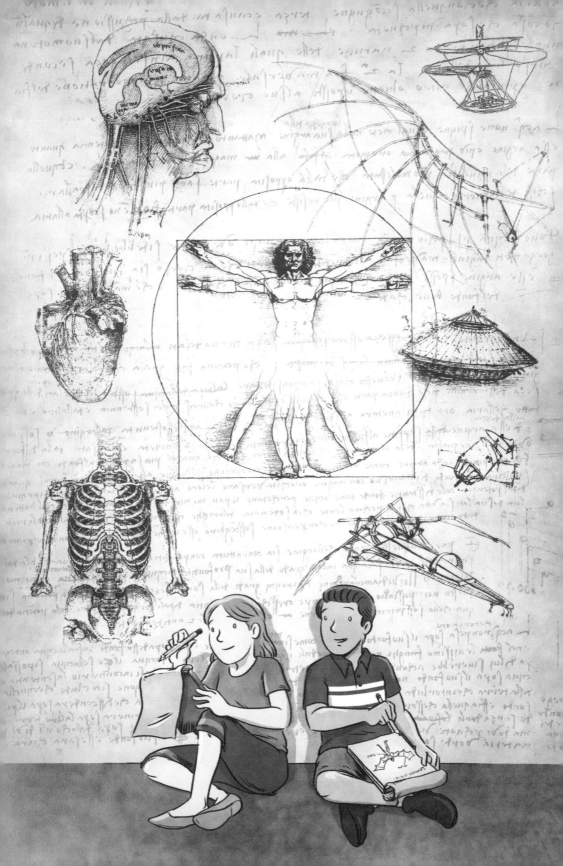

The Tuttles boarded the train to Germany very early the next morning to begin the day-long ride.

Mr. Tuttle and Emily spent some time using an app to learn a bit of German. While Mrs. Tuttle read more from her book, Ethan worked on the online math course he had started over the summer.

"You're already learning that?!" Mrs. Tuttle said, looking over his shoulder. "They don't teach that for another two years at school..."

"Then I guess it's not so bad that I'm missing class," Ethan replied. "I can't wait to learn more algebra so I can learn how to crack codes!"

Mrs. Tuttle squeezed his hand in support. "I'm very proud of you," she said. "It's one thing to learn fun things on a trip like this, but mastering something challenging takes hard work and dedication."

After a few taps on her dad's phone, Emily grinned broadly. "*Herzlichen Glückwunsch!*" she tried to pronounce. It was German for "congratulations!"

Mr. Tuttle had planned several stops in Germany to see sites from World War II, which the twins had recently learned about.

First they visited the Reichstag, which used to be Germany's parliament building. The family had learned that when it caught fire, Adolf Hitler blamed it on Germany's enemies to scare people into giving him all the power he wanted to defeat anyone who stood in his way.

"I used to wonder why so many people supported bad guys," Emily said at a museum showing how the Nazis educated German youth. "Now I know it's because of propaganda, like Mr. Gatto said."

Mrs. Tuttle somberly nodded. "Like many of the other places we've been visiting, a few people with bad ideas have changed the course of history in very bad ways," she said. "That's why it's important that we think for ourselves, learn what is right, and speak out when we notice bad ideas."

The next morning the family got things ready for their drive to Sweden. But before leaving Germany, they made a quick detour to do some family history—stopping by the home Mrs. Tuttle's great-great grandparents had built and lived in.

"These are the same flowers that Mr. Gatto gave us!" Ethan noticed. A small plaque by the sidewalk read "*Vergissmeinnicht*." Emily's app said the flower was called a "forget-me-not" in English.

Ethan and Emily chased each other through the flowers, arms spread wide to soak in the sun.

51

"I'm so glad I'm not sitting at a desk!" Emily said. "Imagine what our friends are doing right now..."

"We don't have to imagine it," Ethan replied matter-of-factly. "We've lived it."

"*Stehen bleiben!*" a policeman suddenly shouted.

"I think he said to stop," Emily whispered to Ethan.

The officer quickly realized they were tourists. "Sorry," he said in English to Mr. and Mrs. Tuttle. "All German children must be in school during the day. So I thought your children were breaking the law by being out here."

That night at the hotel in Sweden, Ethan was still a bit shaken up about the police encounter. "So it's illegal for kids in Germany to do homeschooling instead of going to a government school?"

"Yes, unfortunately..." Mr. Tuttle replied. "They can't here in Sweden, either. In some countries there aren't exceptions to compulsory education like there are where we live."

Mr. Tuttle spoke at his conference the following day, while Mrs. Tuttle and the twins walked through Old Town in Stockholm to shop and relax.

"I feel like I've learned a lot on this trip," Emily said, snacking on cloudberries. "I hope homeschooling will always be like this."

"Going on vacations all the time?" Ethan replied. "Mom and dad would go broke!"

"That's what's great about the freedom to choose," Mrs. Tuttle said. "We can learn about the world by being a part of it rather than being confined in a classroom. And there's plenty to learn right where we live—or through the Internet!"

It had been weeks since the Tuttles sat at their own breakfast table together. As Emily walked over, she saw the fully blossomed flowers near the window.

"The forget-me-nots look so pretty!" she said, bringing the pot to the table. "Now they remind me of our awesome trip."

"It's funny that Mr. Gatto gave us that type of flower," Mr. Tuttle commented. "I think he didn't want us to forget how education really works."

"I'm not going to forget how we almost got arrested!" Ethan said with a mischievous smile. "I can't wait to tell all my friends!"

"It's been fun to focus more on what I want to learn about," Emily added, "rather than having to only study what somebody else says I should."

"I think Mr. Gatto's analogy works," Mrs. Tuttle said. "Letting other people mold you like clay into their version of who you should be is not in your best interest. You should have the freedom to sprout into whatever you are meant to become."

"So, what kind of environment would be best for our new educational adventure?" Mr. Tuttle asked as he spread lingonberry jam on his Swedish pancakes.

The family brainstormed ideas: a quiet reading room, classical music for when they wanted to write, comfortable chairs, and family reading time to learn together.

Then they thought about resources: articles, tutors, courses, online videos, access to the library, lots of field trips, mentors they could learn from, groups of local homeschooling families, and more.

"Seems like we have the start of a good plan," Mrs. Tuttle said. "This is exciting!"

"Yeah, but there's just one thing missing," Ethan said, a slight grin starting to form.

"What's that?" Mr. Tuttle wondered.

"The first and most important rule," he replied. "No homework!"

The End

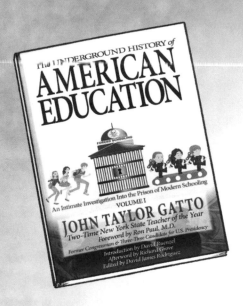

> "I feel ashamed that so many of us cannot imagine a better way to do things than locking children up all day in cells instead of letting them grow up knowing their families, mingling with the world, assuming real obligations, striving to be independent and self-reliant and free."
>
> —John Taylor Gatto

John Taylor Gatto was a school teacher for 30 years. His unique style and deep care for his students brought him accolades and awards, including New York State Teacher of the Year, the latest of which came in the same year that he quit. In an op-ed for the *Wall Street Journal*, he wrote that he no longer wished to "hurt kids to make a living."

A prolific writing and speaking career emerged, where Gatto's sharp wit and exposé of modern schooling created a tidal wave of interest in alternative education methods, with a particular emphasis on homeschooling.

His book, *The Underground History of American Education*, is a critique of modern schooling and a call for something better which avoids the devious intentions of the architects of today's educational institutions.

The Author

Connor Boyack is president of Libertas Institute, a free market think tank in Utah. In that capacity he has changed a significant number of laws in favor of personal freedom and free markets, and has launched a variety of educational projects, including The Tuttle Twins children's book series. Connor is the author of over a dozen books.

A California native and Brigham Young University graduate, Connor currently resides in Lehi, Utah, with his wife and two children.

The Illustrator

Elijah Stanfield is owner of Red House Motion Imaging, a media production company in Washington.

A longtime student of Austrian economics, history, and the classical liberal philosophy, Elijah has dedicated much of his time and energy to promoting the ideas of free markets and individual liberty. Some of his more notable works include producing eight videos in support of Ron Paul's 2012 presidential candidacy. He currently resides in Richland, Washington, with his wife April and their six children.

Contact us at TuttleTwins.com!

Glossary of Terms

Compulsory education: A legal requirement by governments that force parents to send their children to school.

Conformity: Action or behavior that is deemed proper by a social standard or law.

Conveyor belt: A nickname for the schooling process that treats children as products in a factory to be molded and graded.

Curriculum: The lessons and activities taught to students, often matching standards that a teacher is required to follow.

Free will: The freedom to choose one's own path in life.

Propaganda: Material that is often biased and intended to persuade someone to a point of view, without necessarily revealing the truth.

Social engineering: Molding or manipulating people into thinking and acting in a way that is deemed proper or desirable.

Discussion Questions

1. Why is it important for children to enjoy what they learn?
2. Are schooling and education the same thing?
3. Whatever your education situation, how can it be improved?
4. Is compulsion the right way to achieve an important goal?
5. How is free will connected to a person's education?

Don't Forget the Activity Workbook!

Visit **TuttleTwins.com/EducationWorkbook** to download the PDF and provide your children with all sorts of activities to reinforce the lessons they learned in the book!